How To Get God's Attention

by

Dr. Norvel Hayes

Harrison House
Tulsa, Oklahoma

14 13 12 11   7 6 5 4

How To Get God's Attention
ISBN 1-57794-076-8
Copyright © 1997 by Norvel Hayes
P.O. Box 1379
Cleveland, TN 37311

Published by Harrison House Inc.
P.O. Box 35035
Tulsa, Oklahoma 74153

God Just Filled the Room With His Presence

I was once ministering at a Full Gospel Businessmen's convention in Toronto, Canada as their banquet speaker. When it was about time for me to go to the banquet, I walked to the door with my Bible under my arm. I reached down and took hold of the doorknob, turned it, and tried to pull the door back. All of a sudden, the Spirit of the Lord came on me!

God just filled the room full of His glorious Presence. It happened just all of a sudden! I didn't know He was going to do it. He's done that to me many times in many different places.

I knew from experience with God over the years that He wanted to show me something. But I didn't know what it was. (We have to learn to yield ourselves to Him in times like that.)

So I turned loose of the doorknob, and I pushed the door closed. I went back into the room. I began weeping as the Spirit of God was upon me. I yielded myself to Him and asked, "What do You want, Lord? I love You, Jesus. I praise You, Lord. Help me, Lord, to understand what You want. I'll obey You if You'll tell me. What do You want me to do?"

Faith Without Action Is Dead

All of a sudden the word of the Lord come unto me, saying, "As soon as they introduce you to speak this afternoon, I want you to teach what blind Bartimaeus did that caused Me to heal him."

Let me ask you a question: What have you done lately that would cause God to heal you? You will have to do something. You can't just do nothing.

You might say, "Well, I believe the Lord." Well, believing the Lord is called faith in God. But the Bible says that faith is dead without action. You can tell me all day long that you have faith in God, but you have to add some action to your faith. The Bible says that faith is dead without action. You have to do something! Show God that you believe Him and that you trust Him.

You please the Lord by worshipping Him, by believing Him, and by trusting Him, and you do that with your mouth, your voice. You have to understand that God works with words.

God wrote the Bible for you to believe it. The Bible is for you or anybody else who is in trouble. It is for you or anybody else who wants to go to Heaven.

Because then if you ever get into any kind of trouble — it doesn't matter if it is cancer, blindness, being crippled, or anything else that may be wrong with you — God has given you scripture in the Bible to cover your case. And in some cases, He even shows you what the crippled person did to cause God to heal him.

Faith Is Action

Nearly every time someone is healed, the Bible says in some way, "They came to Me. They came to Me wanting help." The word *came* refers to action. Faith is *action*. When you add action to your faith, your faith comes alive.

Living faith is the only kind of faith that produces anything. You can say very nonchalantly that you believe the Lord, and that's fine. But you may do that for a year and still end up dying! There are a lot of people who have died of cancer, saying, "Oh, I believe the Lord. I love God. I've loved God for thirty years. I'm believing the Lord!"

They are not believing the Lord. They say they are, but they are not believing the Lord. Just because a person says he believes the Lord is no sign that he really does.

The Bible says that your faith has a

voice. What you do with your voice shows God whether or not you believe Him.

Someone said, "Well, Brother Norvel, I call Jesus my Healer out loud."

I said, "Hey, that will get the Lord's attention."

"Well, Brother Norvel, I worship the Lord."

I said, "That will get His attention." Worshipping the Lord will get His attention.

"Well, I've been talking to mountains in my life lately, Brother Norvel. I'm telling this cancer, 'You can't kill me, cancer! Jesus is my Healer!'"

I said, "Praise the Lord. You're hitting on pay dirt. You keep on with that, and you're going to get God's attention." *Silent faith does not get God's attention*, even though He loves you.

It Is Up to You

The Bible says when you accept Jesus as your Savior, the Holy Spirit comes in you. He wants to sup with you all the days of your life, and He wants you to sup with Him. And the Bible plainly tells you that God is not a liar. It plainly tells you that once the Holy Spirit comes in you, He will never leave you or never forsake you. And He won't.

But you have to understand that He can also live in you for fifty years and never do very much for you. What the Holy Spirit does for you, all depends on you. It is your choice. It all depends on your mind. It all depends on what kind of decisions you are going to make.

Someone said, "Well, I need a miracle, and I'm going to make the decision that Jesus is my own personal Miracle-worker. Do you think the Lord would like that, Brother Norvel?"

I said, "I know He would."

"Now, with my voice, I'm going to start calling Jesus my Miracle-worker."

I said, "Oh, yeah, He'll like that real well, because He is a Miracle-worker!"

Jesus Is to You Whatever You Call Him

But if you want the Lord Jesus to come to you and be a Miracle-worker to you, then you have to call Him one. Did you know that Jesus becomes to you whatever you call Him? If you curse Him, God will curse you. If you curse the Son of God, God Almighty will curse you.

But if you call Jesus the Savior of your children, and you do it continually, none of your children will ever go to hell.

I am telling you, they won't!

If you call Jesus your Healer, I am telling you boldly that He will come to you and heal you. He will do that if you call Him your Healer.

You say, "Are you going to prove that to us in the Bible?"

Oh yeah, I'm going to prove it to you. And I'm also going to show you what you can do and say to get the Lord's attention so you can receive a miracle from Him or get a healing for your body.

Cause God's Power To Be Released to You

Now back to that story about the word of the Lord that came to me in that hotel room before the banquet. God said, "When you get down there and when they first introduce you today, I want you to teach what blind Bartimaeus did to get Me to heal him. And teach it in a way you've never taught it before! Don't just teach that Jesus is Healer, I want you to teach on what blind Bartimaeus did to get Me to heal him."

The Lord continued, "I had to make the decision to release the healing power to blind Bartimaeus. And I want you to teach on what he did to cause Me to make a decision to release that healing power to him and to give him his eyesight."

Did you know you can *cause* the Lord to release power into you? You can, if you will make the right decision and do what He tells you to do. But if you are going to *cause* Him to do it, you have to please Him first.

So I told the Lord in that hotel room, "Okay, Lord, I will do it." Then the Holy Spirit just lifted off me, and the glory of the Presence of God just began to wane from the room. And then I just turned back into the natural.

So I got my Bible and went downstairs to the banquet. It was totally loaded with people. The room had so many people in it, I couldn't hardly get to the front.

Some of the men were giving their testimony when I arrived at the meeting. I just sneaked in and sat down. I didn't know any of the men on either side of me. I only knew the International Director, who lived in Toronto, and I knew the host.

The gentleman got through testifying, and then the host stood up to speak. He said, "Well, as you know, Mr. Norvel Hayes, a businessman from America, is our banquet speaker this year. But before he comes, I have one more testimony."

The Blind 'Doughnut King'

The host continued, "This man that

you're about to hear is a wealthy man. He made his wealth through selling doughnuts. He has hundreds of doughnut trucks operating out of his doughnut business. They call him the 'Doughnut King' in this part of Canada. And he has become a very, very wealthy man. I'd like for him to come and give a testimony of what the Lord means to him before Norvel Hayes comes and speaks."

So there I am sitting in my chair, and I don't know anyone sitting next to me. Suddenly the guy sitting on my left pushes his chair back to go toward the platform. And I say to myself, *Hmm, I'm sitting next to the 'Doughnut King!'*

This gentleman was a very distinguished-looking businessman. But I noticed that as he stood up, he began to grapple about as he walked slowly toward the platform. I said, "Oh, my God, he's blind! Here is a wealthy man who has millions, and he's blind!"

Jesus is so wonderful; He wanted me to teach on healing so strongly. He wanted me to teach His son what blind Bartimaeus did that caused Him to heal him.

So I'm sitting in the chair, and this man is giving his testimony. This is the first time in my life that anything like this ever happened to me. I am dumbfounded as I think to myself, "Oh, God, let me teach it so he can get it. Help me to teach it strongly so he can get it. I'll be sure to stick to Your Word. That's all I know to do."

'I Want To Heal Him So Much!'

While this man was talking about what the Lord had done for him, suddenly the Holy Ghost began to rise up in me and tears began to stream down my face.

After two or three minutes of those hot tears streaming down my face, I heard words come up out of me so sweetly and so gently. The Lord said, "Son, teach that scripture. Teach it strongly. He loves Me, and I love him. I love him so much because he loves Me. He loves the Gospel." And the Holy Ghost emphasized to me, "I want to give him his eyesight so *much*."

It is important to realize that just because Jesus *wants* to heal you is no sign that He will ever get to do it. He does not heal you *because* He is a Healer and you have a disease; you have to do your part.

Reading the Bible is one thing, but obeying it, confessing it, and claiming it is a different thing altogether.

The Lord said to me in that chair, "I want to heal him so much; he loves Me. He really loves Me!" This man was worth millions and millions of dollars, but his money couldn't buy his eyesight. Yet he loved the Lord. And Jesus wanted to give him his eyesight.

But the Lord *requires* you to believe the Bible. That is the reason God says to you, "I've sent My Word to heal you."

Now you might say, "Well, what does that mean, Brother Norvel? That doesn't mean much to me! I need something specific, not just 'I've sent My Word to heal you'! I have a Bible, I read the Bible, and I believe the Bible, but I'm not healed. What do you mean, 'He sent His Word to heal me'? I read the Bible, but I'm not healed!"

You have to pick out a verse where somebody got healed, and start doing the same thing they did! Many people won't pay the price to get healed; they don't express their faith out loud because of pride.

So the Lord said, "I want to heal him, Son. He loves Me, and I love him." I sat there weeping, I had never heard the Holy Ghost say that to me before in my life! "I want to heal him!"

I don't know how badly you want to get healed, but I can tell you from experience with God that Jesus loves you so much, He wants to heal you a lot more than you want to get healed.

You say, "Well, Brother Norvel, if He does, I love Him and I go to church, and I give money in the offerings, and I believe the Bible. If what you're saying is true, why doesn't He heal me then? I want Him to!" He will as soon as your faith passes His test.

Let's go back to my story about the banquet. The "doughnut king" man got through testifying and sat down. Then they introduced me. I got up knowing I would have to obey the Lord.

It's an awesome thing to think that you might be the difference between a man seeing or being blind the rest of his life. But if you stay in the ministry very long, you find out you win some and lose some. Some people will get healed and some won't get healed, because you can't make people believe the Bible. You can tell them about it, preach it to them, and teach it to them, but you can't make them obey it! You can't make them believe it or confess it.

God Works With Your Words

The Bible only works for you when you confess it. Now God works by His Holy Spirit and the Bible, and sometimes He does do things on His own. But God doesn't promise you that if you get sick,

He will just come to your house and heal you regardless of what you believe.

God basically works one way on the earth with people — He works with words. And He'll work with you with *your* words, not somebody else's words.

The way God blesses me has nothing to do with what God can do for you. You say, "Well, I wish God would bless me the way He does Brother Norvel." He's not going to bless you like that unless you please Him! You have to please Him.

I *call* myself successful. I *call* my bills paid — *all* the time!

The Lord Told Me How To Prosper

I am probably the only man in America (at least that I have ever heard of there may be a lot of people, but I have never heard of one) whose ministry has four churches, all of which are paid for, and we never did take up one offering to pay for any of them.

People ask me, "Brother Norvel, how do you do that?"

Well, the only reason I know how to do it is that the Lord told me how to do it.

I had just bought my first church, and I already had my plans, to print building-fund envelopes; take up offerings; have my own meetings. I was going to pass out my building-fund envelopes and raise my building fund. You know, Christians have *funds* for this and *funds* for that.

I had bought a block of property downtown with a beautiful historical building, and I had only paid twenty thousand dollars down on it. The wealthy people who had built it didn't want it torn down. They wanted me to buy it.

The First Methodist Church owned it. The building had a sanctuary with four rows of pews, chandeliers, and thirty-eight hand-painted, stained-glass windows, worth about a hundred thousand dollars. It also had an educational building with twenty-five offices. It was just absolutely gorgeous the way it was built and furnished.

Right after I bought that building, I was speaking one night at RHEMA Bible Training Center in Broken Arrow, Oklahoma. All of a sudden, the Spirit of the Lord came on me, and about four or five hundred people jumped up out of their seat and ran down front before I could even stop them, falling on the floor and crying.

The glory of the Lord came in and lasted about fifteen minutes. I was on the stage by myself, with Brother Kenneth

Hagin sitting down in the front. All of a sudden, I looked around, and he was on the stage walking up and down. We would pass each other. I walked one way praying in the Spirit, and he walked the other way praying in the Spirit.

After about thirty minutes had gone by, I stopped him and said, "Brother Hagin, I'm not going to do anything else. The Holy Ghost has done what He wants to do. I'm not going to give any type of an invitation now. If you want to do anything, feel free to do it."

He said, "No, no, no. No, the Holy Ghost has done it."

I said, "Well, whenever you want to close out, you just feel free; you obey the Lord."

He said, "Okay."

So we made a few more trips back and forth on the platform. Then he took a microphone and started staggering. I grabbed him and sat him down in the chair. He said, "In all of my ministry, this is only the fourth time that prophecy has ever moved upon me this deeply." Those were his words.

And Brother Hagin started prophesying. He prophesied about forty-five minutes. Glory to God! It was like another chapter being written in the Bible.

And during that forty-five minutes, he prophesied to me two different times. One time the Holy Ghost said, "Norvel Hayes, from this night forward, I'm making a change in your ministry. It's going to change into mass altar calls. What you saw tonight before your eyes while you were speaking will happen to you many times in the future of your ministry. I'll require you to give mass altar calls, and people will come to the altar by the masses! And when they do this, I will move upon them supernaturally." Then Brother Hagin went on and started prophesying something else.

After a while, he called my name and prophesied to me again. Now this is in front of about twenty-two hundred people. The prophet said to me in the Holy Ghost, "Norvel Hayes, I want to say unto you, son, that you have obeyed Me, and I am pleased with your Bible college. Your Bible college is in My perfect will. And the building you just bought..."

Now I had in the back of my mind my plans about the building fund envelopes and all kinds of things. I was going to raise money that way, because I didn't know anything else.

And the Lord said through Brother Hagin, "The building you just bought was in My perfect will, and I want you to keep on going out in the field to teach the people. I am going to take care of the building; don't you worry about it at all. Just thank Me, because I am going to pay for the building."

I had paid twenty thousand dollars down on it, and I was thinking like this: What about my building envelopes? What about the building fund I was going to open up? Should I still do that, or did that prophecy blow that idea?

The Lord said, "Just thank Me for it, because I'm going to pay for it."

I said, "Well, that's the easiest thing I ever heard in my life."

Thanking God for the Money Coming In

So after that meeting, every time I went to visit that building, I would lay my hands on it as I left and say, "Thank you Lord, for sending the money in to pay for this building!"

I never did take up one offering to pay for the building — not one! I just started thanking the Lord for it. I said, "Thank You, Lord, for sending the money in to pay for this building!"

We had financed the building for three years. I had enough faith in my building fund that I could pay for this building in three years. I started thanking God for it, and the money started coming. I never did take up an offering, nor did I have a building fund. But the money started coming in.

When it came in, I would take a big check to the First Methodist Church and give it to the pastor. I would go back in a few days or weeks later and give him another big check.

All kinds of things were happening. People would come in and say, "Brother Norvel, I was in West Virginia praying, and the Lord told me to come down here and give you this check for your Bible college." And they'd give me a check for thousands of dollars.

I would say, "Well, I believe it!"

I had the money to pay the thing off in a year and a half, just by thanking the Lord.

Spend Time Thanking God

Did you know everything you thank God for, He'll give it to you? That is one of the things that bogs down Christians and bogs down the church. It will bog your finances down, too, if you don't spend enough time thanking God for your finances or if you lean over to your own understanding.

"Well, I have my plans, and I have this and I have that. And I'm going to call this guy to come speak who takes up big offerings, because I'm behind on my payments."

But you don't need that guy to come in and take up a big offering for you; you just need to bombard Heaven with thanksgiving several times a day. You just need to call that account paid with your mouth and then thank the Lord *for* it, and let the Lord hear you several thousand times. *After* God hears your thanksgiving several thousand times, you will get His attention.

"Well, Brother Norvel, I thanked the Lord four or five times last week." Oh, really? No. The Lord said when you call upon Him a great deal, you will get His attention.

Just because Jesus heals people is no sign that you will ever get your healing. You can get it, but only if you make the right kind of decision. If I can talk you into pleasing Him, I will guarantee you that you will get your healing when your faith pleases Him.

Your Faith Has a Voice

After you get healed, Jesus will say, "Your faith healed you." I bet you thought He healed people just because

He was Jesus. No, no, no. Read the Bible, and you will find out. Your *faith* heals you.

The kind of faith that heals you is faith that has a voice. It has the voice of asking. It has the voice of mercy. It has the voice of victory! It has the voice of crying out! You cry out a great deal to make contact with Him. Any human being living on the face of the earth can make contact with God! Cry out that your crooked legs will be stretched out to be made normal. Cry out for new kidneys!

You say, "Well, I'm going to go to that meeting where they're anointed to pray for me." Well, that's fine, you might get healed that way, but you might not. But with this way of faith, there is no "might-nots." It's for everybody.

The Faith of Blind Bartimaeus

So now let's get back to that blind man at the banquet. I have a millionaire blind man sitting over here, and the Holy Ghost wants to give him his eyesight. And the Lord told me to teach about blind Bartimaeus real strongly.

And they came to Jericho: and as he went out of Jericho with his disciples and a great number of people, blind Bartimaeus, the son of Timaeus, sat by the highway

side begging. And when he heard that it was Jesus of Nazareth, he began to cry out...

Mark 10:46

It said, the *blind* man began to cry out! The first thing out of the blind man's mouth was, *"Jesus!"*

When you're alone, that's what you're going to have to do. If you want to hear from Heaven, if you want to be healed, or if you want a miracle, you're going to have to cry out, 'Jesus!' You're going to have to approach Him in the right way. There is no other name mentioned by which you might get to Heaven or be healed or receive a miracle. Only the name of Jesus. You might as well know this; it's Jesus or nothing.

In all aspects of life — finances, getting your children saved, receiving a healing or a miracle — it's either Jesus or nothing. Make up your mind to that. Learn something from this scripture. When you open up your mouth to get help, call out His name first.

Listen to what blind Bartimaeus said: **...Jesus, thou son of David, have mercy on me (Mark 10:47).**

The Bible says in verse 48, **...and many charged....** Now the word *many* is the opposite of a few. The word *charged* is different than walking over and talking to someone gently and sweetly. Charged means like a bull south of the border charging the matador: **And many charged him that he should hold his peace...** (Mark 10:48).

"Be quiet, you old blind man! Shut up! The Master passeth by!"

Remember what I said earlier: Faith with a voice combined with action gets God's attention. Now notice blind Bartimaeus bypassed all men, even when they tried to shut him up: **...but he cried the more a great deal...** (Mark 10:48).

A *great deal* is opposite from a little bit. The Bible says that blind Bartimaeus cried out a "great deal." That's the opposite of most Christians, because most Christians will just do it a little bit — a few times.

Stay With It

But nearly all Christians will get tired of doing what they are supposed to do to get God's attention after two or three weeks. And most of the time, they won't do it a great deal even during that two or three weeks; they will only do what they are supposed to do a little bit. But after about two to four weeks, their faith just kind of winds down, just like when you spin a top and it spins for a while and then starts winding down until it falls.

But the Bible will never spin down. The Bible is not a top. Your faith is not supposed to be like a top that wears out. Your faith is alive all the time. And the only kind of faith that ever works is faith with a voice, faith with authority, and faith that is alive and full of action. That is the only kind of faith that works for you. And blind Bartimaeus had it.

The people who walked with Jesus didn't have that kind of faith, because they charged blind Bartimaeus to shut up. "Shut up, blind man, hold your peace! The Master passes by."

Blind Bartimaeus says, "Well, is that right? The Master is the One I'm trying to get to. Hey, Jesus, have mercy on me!"

"I said, be quiet, hold your peace! Shut up!"

"Jesus, have mercy on me! JESUS, HAVE MERCY ON ME!"

The Bible said that Bartimaeus cried out a great deal. That means lots of times — *right in their face.*

"Well, Brother Norvel, the church I go to, they wouldn't let me do that."

Well, go under a tree and do it! Your pastor is not under that tree. If they won't let you cry out to Jesus in faith in your church, go under a tree and do it. Do it at home. I know you can't interrupt services all the time. But you can do it when they get through. God is patient; you can wait.

But notice what happens to blind Bartimaeus:

> ...Thou son of David, have mercy on me. And Jesus stood still...

> **Mark 10:48,49**

Notice that Jesus stood still *after* blind Bartimaeus cried out a great deal, or many times, right in the front of people, with no shame. He just kept crying out. Then the Lord Jesus Christ stopped walking and stood still! He opened up His mouth and said, "I command you to bring that man to Me, that one crying out."

"Oh Lord, which man?"

"What do you mean, which man? The one who is crying out! The one whose faith I hear!"

Faith has a voice! A loud, victory-type voice.

> ...Jesus stood still, and commanded him to be called. And they call the blind man, saying unto him, Be of good

comfort, rise; he calleth thee.

And he, casting away his garment, rose, and came to Jesus.

And Jesus answered and said unto him, What wilt thou that I should do unto thee?...

Mark 10:49-51

Someone might say, "Brother Norvel, didn't Jesus know Bartimaeus was blind?"

Yes, but the Bible says you have not because you ask not. God likes for you to ask for things.

...The blind man said unto him, Lord, that I might receive my sight.

And Jesus said unto him, Go thy way; thy FAITH hath made thee whole. And immediately he received his sight, and followed Jesus in the way.

Mark 10:51,52

Immediately Bartimaeus received his sight. Jesus told him, "Your *faith* has caused you to receive sight! Your faith has healed you!"

Now remember that millionaire blind man? After my message, I said to him,

28

"Your faith can heal you, if your faith will be like blind Bartimaeus' faith. But you have to cry out. Blind Bartimaeus cried out, 'Jesus, Son of David, have mercy on me!' Not just three or four times, but a great deal, which means many times, and with a loud voice!

"And He will hear anybody! The cries of a broken heart, the cries of a blind man, the Lord God will hear anybody. And the Lord will hear your cries. It doesn't make a difference what's wrong with you; He will hear your cries."

I would even pause after I'd say it, to give him plenty of time to think about what I was saying.

Well, this blind millionaire didn't cry out. Sometimes rich people won't cry out in public like that. He didn't cry out. And they led him out of the building, still blind.

Have Blind Bartimaeus' Kind of Faith

Your faith can please the Lord, if you have the same kind of faith that blind Bartimaeus had. Blind Bartimaeus' faith healed him. Jesus said, "Your faith has healed you." His cries were cries of faith. He cried "a great deal with a loud voice." That was blind Bartimaeus' faith.

Beating a tin pan at the side of the

road and crying out, "Help the blind!" is not faith. That's a little natural faith to get somebody's attention who is walking by.

Well, blind Bartimaeus was sick and tired of beating the pan and yelling, "Help the blind!." And *you* probably won't ever be healed until you get sick and tired of that dumb disease that is trying to mess you up.

The bad news was that the people helped the millionaire blind man out of the room. He did not receive his eyesight, because he refused to do what blind Bartimaeus did.

I hope that you will listen to the Lord Jesus Christ when He tells you that faith has a voice. I hope you will listen to the Lord Jesus Christ when He told blind Bartimaeus, "Your faith has healed you." All Jesus did was heard Bartimaeus' faith when he cried out, "Jesus...son of David, have mercy on me."

I honestly believe you can sit in your living room and say, "Jesus, the true living Son of God, You are my Healer! Jesus, I want to thank You for healing me! Have mercy on me, Lord; You're my Healer!" And if you will do that a great deal, I actually believe that you will get God's attention, and the healing power of

God will come into your house and just give you a healing.

But the Lord God said, "If you want to please Me, obey Me and show Me that you're not ashamed of Me in front of men."

If you want to be healed, obey the Lord. Get on your knees before God and cry out, "*Jesus*, have mercy on me! *Jesus*, have mercy on me!" And say it over and over again, a great deal. It only works if you do it a great deal — lots of times. That is pleasing to the Lord.

Now blind Bartimaeus' faith was his mouth — what he cried out to Jesus. Your faith is what you say with your mouth. The highest type of faith that you have is what you confess that Jesus is. That's the highest type of faith in the world. You confess what you believe that Jesus is.

Confess What Jesus Is to You

Always remember to confess what Jesus is to you. Say, "Jesus, have mercy on me. Jesus, I confess that You are my Healer. I confess that You are healing me now. Your healing power is a gift to the church, and Your healing power is going down through my body driving out all affliction in Jesus' Name. Thank You, Lord, for healing me."

If you'll talk like that to Him and

confess that, His healing power will go right down through your body in a few days or a few weeks, or whenever your faith pleases the Lord.

When your faith pleases the Lord on the same level that blind Bartimaeus' faith pleased Him, you'll get His attention. And He will listen to your voice. The Bible tells you in no uncertain terms that if you will just keep on and on crying out to Jesus for what you want, He will hear you; He will give it to you.

I got it straight from the Holy Ghost, straight from the throne of God, that the Holy Ghost loves you that much. God made you. He made your face, He made your lips, He made your voice, and He so desires to hear from you. And if you'll keep on and on, calling Jesus your Healer and tell Him that you believe by His stripes you are healed, the Lord God Almighty will heal you. His healing power will come to you.

HARRISON HOUSE
P.O. Box 35035
Tulsa, OK 74153

Made in the USA
Monee, IL
08 July 2026